J.M.W. TURNER

MICHAEL KITSON

J. M. W. Turner

BLANDFORD PRESS
LONDON

editor: Anthony Bosman
lay-out: Wim van Stek
first published in an English edition in 1964
by Blandford Press Ltd., London
© 1964 and printed in Holland by The Ysel Press Ltd, Deventer

Turner is perhaps more difficult to assess fairly than any other major British artist. Neither in his own time nor in ours has he seemed to fit conveniently into a niche. His contemporaries were both overwhelmed and baffled by him. Conservative critics attacked him; the Royal Academy supported him; he had great influence on the young. Yet while everybody acknowledged his genius he could persuade patrons to buy only his most conventional pictures—and from these he made a fortune. Even Ruskin, Turner's warmest and most intelligent admirer, probably did as much to obscure as to clarify the true nature of his art.

Opinion today is passing through a transitional stage. Among various artists and critics there are signs of a livelier interest in Turner than at any time during the past fifty years. The great collection of his paintings at the Tate Gallery is in course of being cleaned and re-hung; books are once more being written about him; scholars are re-investigating special aspects of his work. But these are quite recent developments. Not long ago Turner was the white elephant of British painting—all but ignored by historians of the subject and admired only by a handful of enthusiasts for what were partly the wrong reasons. To the historian Turner was, and to some extent still is, a puzzle. Lacking both the manifest "Englishness" of Constable and Constable's relationship to the mainstream of nineteenth-century landscape painting in France, he was difficult to place; while critics whose taste had been formed on classical models, as Sir Kenneth Clark has pointed out, found his work undisciplined and diffuse and his magic unconvincing.

To his admirers, on the other hand, it was precisely the magician in Turner that appealed. He was the sorcerer who, after

discarding the cumbersome apparatus of earlier landscape painters which he had used in his youth, went on in later life to
conjure up out of air, light and colour those dazzling visions
nominally entitled "Norham Castle" or "Interior at Petworth"
(pp. 62, 63) that are now his most popular pictures. But there
is more to Turner than sleight-of-hand, however brilliant, and
more than can be gathered by examining only his later work,
even though that work undoubtedly embodied his most important contribution to nineteenth-century art.

Viewed as a whole, his career exhibits a restless energy, an
unceasing capacity for invention, that is unique among English
artists; to find a parallel for it in this country it is necessary to
compare him with poets, novelists and social critics rather than
with other painters. He was at once the most traditional artist
of his time and the most original: traditional in his devotion to
the Old Masters and to the aesthetic ideals of the eighteenth
century; original in his creation of new styles that radically
undermined the normal conventions of picture-making. He
believed in the time-honoured role of the artist as poet—but
knocked away the foundations on which previous poetic
painting had been built. He evolved a highly personal artistic
language of his own, risking incomprehensibility in the process
—yet did so in the name of doctrines largely contained in the
Discourses on Art of Sir Joshua Reynolds.

Free forms, a network of interlacing brush-strokes, an overall
treatment of the picture surface in terms of broad areas of light
and colour—these are the outstanding characteristics of Turner's
mature and late style. It has sometimes been said that he prepar-
ed the way for the Impressionists by this, and it may be true
that Monet was influenced by him when painting similar subjects, such as views of the Thames or Venice. But, fundamental-
ly, what Turner succeeded in creating for the nineteenth century
was not so much a foretaste of Impressionism as an alternative
to Impressionism—an alternative which the nineteenth century
could not absorb but which has come to seem increasingly
relevant in more recent times.

In some ways, "Norham Castle" (p. 62) or "Interior at Petworth" (p. 63) or—to take two further examples—the "Seascape" illustrated on p. 69 and "Shade and Darkness: the Evening of the Deluge" (p. 72), with its central vortex and surrounding rings of colour, have more in common with American abstract painting of the 1950's than with the tranquil, intimate landscapes of Monet or Pissarro. There will be occasion to return to this comparison later.

But if Turner's art is mysterious, his character and the basic pattern of his career are straightforward enough. He was a small, tough, taciturn man, uncouth and ill at ease in society but charming when in the company of sympathetic and unpretentious people.

Contrary to what some of his contemporaries thought, he was neither a miser nor ungenerous by temperament, but he drove a hard bargain with patrons and charged high prices for the landscapes he sold. He also earned a regular income by working for publishers of engravings of picturesque views. In fact, he made a considerable fortune from his work, although he lost part of it as a result of unwise speculation in stocks and shares.

He lived frugally, even squalidly, saving his money for his annual tours. He never married, but kept mistresses and was rumoured to have several illegitimate children. But while the disreputable side of his life should not be glossed over, there is no need to exaggerate its importance.

He lived essentially for his art. As an artist he was precocious, industrious, business-like and incredibly energetic. He was not introspective, as Constable was, nor what would nowadays be called an intellectual; but he was highly intelligent, as his contemporaries and Ruskin always insisted.

He was blessed with enviable facility (again unlike Constable) but his work was never facile. Most important of all, he had outstanding powers of visual concentration. He could *see* faster and more clearly than most people and fix the impression of what he had seen indelibly on his mind. He had something of

7

that intense clarity of vision that we associate with one of his contemporaries who was otherwise very different from him: William Blake. But whereas Blake claimed to see "through" not "with" the eye, Turner saw with the natural eye alone; his vision was essentially optical.

There are many anecdotes concerning Turner's capacity for concentration. Stories are told of him sketching out of doors undistracted by the attentions of onlookers or appalling weather conditions; putting his head out of a railway carriage window during a shower of rain to observe an effect used for "Rain, Steam and Speed" (p. 71); having himself lashed to the mast of the Ariel packet-boat to record the storm depicted in "Snowstorm: Steamboat off a Harbour's Mouth Making Signals in Shallow Water" (p. 68). ("I did not paint it to be *understood*," he told the Rev. W. Kingsley, "but I wished to show what such a scene was like.")

On varnishing days at the Royal Academy he would arrive very early in the morning bearing a wet canvas smeared with a few broad strokes of transparent colour, set it up on the wall, work steadily without talking or allowing himself to be interrupted until it was finished, then walk away as silently as he had come. It is notable that almost all these insights into Turner's working methods and habits are provided by other people. Unlike Constable, he was hardly ever revealing about himself.

Joseph Mallord William Turner (known as William or Bill to his family, but usually referred to only by his initials and surname today) was born in London on the 23rd April 1775. He was two months younger than Thomas Girtin, fourteen months older than Constable. His father was a barber. Father and son remained devoted to each other until the father's death in 1829; for many years the father had looked after his son's business affairs and his gallery.

While Turner was a boy the family lived in Maiden Lane, Covent Garden. He remained a Londoner all his life. In 1799 he moved up in the world and took lodgings at the corner of

Harley Street and Queen Anne Street; this, and later another, adjoining house to which he added a gallery, was his town headquarters. He also lived for part of the year at one time or another at Hammersmith, in a house next to Syon House (Isleworth) and finally at Chelsea. From one of these houses he would set off in the summer of each year on a sketching tour somewhere in the British Isles or abroad.

He had only a brief schooling and began drawing as a boy. According to the diarist Joseph Farington, he was apprenticed for a time to Thomas Malton, a topographical watercolourist who specialized in architectural subjects. In 1789 he entered the Royal Academy Schools and in 1790 (at the age of fifteen) showed for the first time at the summer exhibition; his contribution was a watercolour of the Archbishop's Palace, Lambeth. His style was precociously accomplished and his success rapid. In 1799 he was made an Associate of the Royal Academy at the earliest permissible age — twenty-four. In 1802 he was elected a full Academician "in the room of Francis Wheatley, Esq., deceased."

The Academy supported Turner all his life against the attacks of the connoisseurs and the more conservative critics; he himself reciprocated by being one of its most devoted members, serving frequently on the hanging committee and the council. In 1807 he was elected "Professor of Perspective", though he managed to postpone giving his first lecture until 1811. He gave a series of six lectures fairly regularly until 1819, then gradually they lapsed until he finally resigned the appointment in 1838. We shall refer later to the subject matter of one of these lectures, that entitled "Backgrounds: Introduction of Architecture and Landscape".

Turner made his name as a painter of topographical watercolours of picturesque subjects. Here, as so often, he seized on an existing trend rather than created a new one; equally characteristically, he exploited it more vigorously and thoroughly than anyone else. The interest he was reflecting was the fashion for touring the remoter parts of the British Isles in order to

9

admire the scenery and compare it with the work of famous painters, notably Claude Lorrain, Gaspard Poussin and Salvator Rosa. A considerable literature had grown up around this vogue, and to "make the tour" of the Lakes, the Peak District or North Wales had become a fashionable summer occupation.

At the same time there was an awakening antiquarian interest in English mediaeval remains—castles, ruined abbeys and the Gothic cathedrals. Often the two enthusiasms—picturesque and antiquarian—were combined. By the 1780's artists such as Thomas Hearne, Michael "Angelo" Rooker and Edward Dayes had begun the practice of making regular sketching expeditions to famous beauty spots, and engravings after their work were often used as illustrations to guide books and historical surveys of mediaeval architecture.

This, then, was the environment in which Turner began his career. Between 1791 and 1802 he visited Bristol, South Wales, Monmouthshire, Herefordshire, North Wales, Kent, Derbyshire, Lincoln, Ely, Cambridge, the Isle of Wight, Northumberland, the Lake District, Wiltshire and the Lowlands of Scotland. His watercolour style at this period was very close to that of his friend and contemporary, Thomas Girtin (died 1802). For several years (c. 1794-97) the two artists often worked together side by side in the evenings at the house of a Dr. Monro, copying watercolours for him by John Robert Cozens. Girtin, too, specialized in picturesque subjects and landscape views; he was also partly responsible for the final liberation of the watercolour medium from its former subservience to monochrome drawing. But while Girtin's later work undoubtedly made a distinct and influential contribution to English art, it seems likely that, during the "Monro" period, it was Turner's style that was the more advanced of the two.

In such a watercolour as "Tintern Abbey" (p. 38), exhibited at the Academy in 1794, Turner displays his interest not only in the architectural features of the building but also in its picturesque qualities. He chooses a low viewpoint so as to show up the tracery against the sky; two figures appear at the bottom left to fix the scale of the drawing; light and shade are used—light at the bottom, shade at the top—to create a mood of mystery and romance.

Another watercolour (p. 21), also technically close to some of Girtin's though dating from a few years later, shows Turner's mastery of a more rural type of subject matter: cows drinking at a pool beneath trees with a meadow and a view of Fonthill Abbey in the distance. Despite the greater realism of its execution, this too is not an entirely objective rendering of the motif, for it is imbued with that meditative feeling for the beauties of ordinary nature which characterized English landscape painting of this period.

Apart from Girtin, the strongest influence on Turner's early watercolour style was that of John Robert Cozens. "From Cozens he drew his first taste for the poetry of landscape and his special qualities of infinity, distance and aerial perspective", wrote his biographer, Thornbury. Cozens was noted for his watercolours of the Swiss Alps, several of which Turner had actually copied; it is not surprising that when he visited Switzerland for the first time in 1802 he saw the Alps to some extent through Cozens's eyes.

Ever since 1793, the Continent had been closed to English travellers owing to the war with France, but with the signing of the short-lived Peace of Amiens (March 1802-May 1803), artists and others seized the opportunity to cross the Channel. Turner set out on the 15th July, going first straight through Paris to Switzerland. In Switzerland, as he told Farington on his return, "he saw very fine thunderstorms among the mountains—fragments and precipices very romantic and strikingly grand". Farington also recorded about this time that "Turner has no settled process but drives the colour about until he has expressed the idea in his mind"—a procedure which recalls Alexander Cozens's use of improvised "blots" to assist the imagination when making landscape drawings.

Nevertheless, the immediate results of Turner's first visit to the Alps were disappointing. Although he was clearly exhilarated by the scenery, he seems not to have known quite what to do with it at first. He took refuge, as it were, in the production of large numbers of rather dry monochrome drawings (p. 40), from which he afterwards made a few finished watercolours for his friend and patron, Walter Fawkes of Farnley Hall; these watercolours were not entirely successful, either, since they were too brown in tone and too large in scale for the medium. It was not until several years later that Turner was able to absorb his Alpine experiences and put them to good use in his work. (There was a similar "delayed reaction" after his first visit to Italy in 1819.) Artistically, the finest products of the Swiss tour of 1802 were a small group of drawings in opaque watercolour on grey paper, of which the "Mer de Glace: View of Chamounix with Blair's Hut" (p. 23) is an example. Such drawings were probably not done, or at least not finished, directly from nature but were worked up in the evening in the artist's hotel room. Executed with broad strokes of the brush in white and grey-green, they are extremely beautiful and capture the rarified, icy atmosphere of the Alps with marvellous skill.

The second object of Turner's Continental tour of 1802 was to visit the Louvre in Paris. Here he saw the great collection of Old Master paintings which Napoleon had looted during his campaigns in Italy and also, of course, the pictures from the French royal collections which were now on public view. In two or three weeks he filled a notebook with studies, some of them coloured, of pictures he thought important. The latter were chiefly works in which landscape played a major, but not necessarily exclusive, part in the composition.

To judge from the number of studies devoted to their work in the notebook, the artists who most attracted Turner's attention in the Louvre were Titian, Poussin and Rembrandt. He also made extensive written comments on the pictures, discriminating perceptively between what he considered to be their merits and defects. He used all this material later for his own pictures and lectures.

More than this, Turner's visit to the Louvre confirmed and deepened his interest in a wider problem: that of "historic landscape", i.e., landscape treated in a grand or epic style with subject matter drawn from the Bible, classical history or myth. Hitherto, seventeenth-century Dutch marine painting had been the chief Old Master influence on his work. His first oil painting had been a seascape exhibited in 1796. At the Academy of 1801 he had scored a "succès d'éstime" with another seascape (p. 22), commissioned by the Duke of Bridgewater and modelled partly on a painting already belonging to the Duke by William van de Velde. Turner followed the Dutchman's example closely in this work, especially in his treatment of light and shade; light forms are silhouetted against dark, and dark against light, to give an overall tonal balance to the composition.

The most notable difference lies in the emphasis which Turner gives to the contrast between the tilted boat in the foreground and the motionless ships on the horizon; the latter are placed parallel to the picture surface with their masts and spars out-lined against the sky. These calm, fixed points act as a foil to the movement of the smaller boat, emphasizing its heaving, rocking motion all the more. Turner often made use of such contrasts: sometimes a dynamic form counterbalanced by a static one, as here; at other times a sharp, precise accent set off against a misty, amorphous background.

In 1800 he exhibited the first of his large Biblical epics, the so-called "Fifth Plague of Egypt" (John Herron Art Museum, Indianapolis) and in 1802 the "Tenth Plague of Egypt", just before his departure for Switzerland. In or about 1804 he executed a similar picture, "The Destruction of Sodom" (detail, p. 24).

All three paintings show some influence from both Nicolas and Gaspard Poussin, whose work Turner is known to have studied in England even before he visited Paris. Heroic but bizarre grandeur is the most obvious characteristic of these pictures; they are conspicuous for what Constable stigmatized as "bravura—an attempt to do something beyond the truth."

They also contain a strong element of the theatrical. Lights flash and colours glow in a manner that recalls De Loutherbourg's "Eidophusikon" rather than the classic harmonies of Nicolas Poussin. The "Eidophusikon" was a popular entertainment consisting of moving scenery and coloured lights with sound effects—a sort of late eighteenth-century "son et lumière"— which De Loutherbourg put on at a London theatre when Turner was a boy.

Theatrical or not, however, the two "Plagues of Egypt" and the "Destruction of Sodom" were certainly examples of "historic landscape". It would be untrue to say that there was a general vogue for such landscapes at this time, for not many had yet been painted. But ever since the exhibition of Richard Wilson's "Destruction of Niobe's Children" (Mellon Collection) at the Society of Artists in 1760, the idea of painting imaginary landscapes with historical or mythological subject matter had been present in the minds of English artists. It had even penetrated to the watercolourists, and in 1799 a "Sketching Club" was founded by Girtin for the purpose of "establishing by practice a School of Historic Landscape—the subjects being original designs from poetick passages."

In a wider sense, this trend can be seen as part of the contemporary cult of the Sublime. The object was to stir the imagination by the use of bold and striking effects and to evoke a fantastic world more awe-inspiring than the world of everyday reality. Reynolds was ultimately behind it, with his advice to artists to devote themselves to employ the historical style when painting figure subjects; he also thought that historical principles might be applied to the lesser genres of portraiture and landscape, although he had some doubts as to whether landscape could be successfully treated in this way in practice.

The Swiss emigré artist, Henry Fuseli, was thinking on similar lines, and indeed went further. Writing of "that last branch of uninteresting subjects—that kind of landscape which is entirely occupied with the tame delineation of a given spot", he contrasted the modern taste for topography with the practice of the Old Masters in terms that might almost have been applied to Turner himself (whom he is said to have called the only landscape painter of genius in Europe): "To them, nature disclosed her bosom in the varied light of rising, meridian, setting suns; in twilight, night and dawn. Height, depth, solitude, strike, terrify, absorb, bewilder in their scenery. We tread on classic or romantic ground, or wander through the characteristic groups of rich congenial objects."

It is interesting to note that Fuseli spoke these words in a lecture at the Academy in 1805; that is to say, after Turner had already begun to paint historic landscapes but before he wrote his own "Backgrounds" lecture. Other landscapes by Turner in this category include "The Deluge" (c. 1805), "Hannibal crossing the Alps" (1812, p. 32), "The Battlefield of Waterloo" (1818) and "The Parting of Hero and Leander" (1837): all these are in the Tate Gallery.

But Turner was not content with only one style of historic landscape. He also painted a "Holy Family" in imitation of Titian in 1803 and a calm Poussinesque composition, "The Gardens of the Hesperides" (both Tate Gallery) in 1806. In 1803 he also began to consider another mode: ideal, or Claudian, landscape. This was to be the most lasting inspiration of all.

"The Festival of the Opening of the Vintage at Macon" (p. 26) was painted in 1803 and remains one of Turner's finest essays in the Claudian manner. It is admirably executed throughout and, although rather dark, beautifully preserved. Typically, it has an invented subject: a romantic projection into the Arcadian past of a picturesque modern festival. Also typical of Turner is the fact that the painting is not a direct copy of one by Claude but a variation, possibly based on one of the two large landscapes by Claude from the Altieri collection which Turner saw when they were first brought to London in 1799.

From then onwards, the image of Claude grew in his mind, not only providing him with direct inspiration from time to time but also acting as a steadying influence on his style as a whole. From about 1807 until his departure for Italy in 1819 he produced an increasing number of calm pictures; he did this in his work in all styles, not only in pictures directly inspired by Claude.

More than this, Claude was the hero of Turner's lecture, "Backgrounds: Introduction of Architecture and Landscape", first delivered in 1811 as the sixth in his series on perspective at the Royal Academy. In this lecture, cast in the form of a discussion of the great masters of landscape painting from Titian to his own time, Turner made the clearest statement in his career of his view of landscape painting and of his own rôle in its history. All along there are echoes of Sir Joshua Reynolds's *Discourses*: idealization of nature, the importance of transcending the local and the particular, the need to appeal to the mind and the imagination, not merely to the eye. Landscapes, like figure subjects, Turner said in effect, should be treated in an elevated style; they should not be just transcriptions of what the artist sees in front of him.

In his own work Turner put these beliefs into practice. Even when drawing or painting views of actual places (as he often did) he tended to ignore or alter local topographical details; as his contemporaries recognized, he was essentially an ideal painter. "He was truly the poet of painting", wrote one of them, Cyrus Redding. And he continued to include a number of ideal or historical landscapes among his contributions to the Royal Academy exhibitions until the end of his life, just as Reynolds had shown two or three historical portraits alongside his more naturalistic and informal works. (In fact, taking Royal Academy exhibitions alone, Turner's work in this category represented a higher proportion of the total than Reynolds's, but Turner produced a greater number of naturalistic paintings and watercolours that were not shown at the Academy, not to mention innumerable sketches that were never meant for sale or exhibition at all.)

In sum, it seems evident that Turner saw himself as trying to do for landscape what Reynolds had attempted to do for portraiture; namely, assimilate it to the great tradition of history painting. Indeed more; Turner seems to have thought that landscape could fulfil most, if not all, the functions that had previously been divided among many different categories of painting: allegory, history (classical, Biblical and modern), portraiture and genre—in addition, of course, to the various sub-categories of landscape itself. His ambition was to be a landscape painter of universal scope.

And just as he had explained his views on landscape painting in words in the "Backgrounds" lecture, so he demonstrated them in visual form in his "Liber Studiorum". This book, inspired by the eighteenth-century engravings after Claude's "Liber Veritatis", was begun in 1806 and continued until 1819. It consisted of engravings in mezzotint issued at an average rate of six a year until 71 were published in all. The subjects were divided into six different kinds or classes, the class to which each belonged being indicated at the head of the plate by an initial: P (Pastoral); EP (Elevated Pastoral); A (Architectural); M (Marine); H (Historical); M or Ms (Mountainous). P. 46 shows one of the Elevated Pastoral subjects and is an example of the direct stylistic influence of the "Liber Veritatis"; the scene on p. 47 belongs to the Mountainous category, in designing which Turner was able to make use of his experiences in Switzerland.

No less interesting is the frontispiece to the "Liber" (p. 44). It has been mentioned earlier that Turner was not what would now be called an intellectual; he was certainly not a radical. In many ways he was a straightforward British patriot, exulting in British victories during the Napoleonic Wars and fascinated by modern scientific and industrial achievements. On the other hand, he was profoundly pessimistic about the final outcome of all human endeavour.

In the catalogue entries for his pictures at the Academy exhibitions he would print extracts from a manuscript poem of his own composition entitled, significantly, "The Fallacies of Hope". He was haunted by the "fate of empire": proud that the supremacy of Great Britain should be founded on ideals of

17

liberty, with which he contrasted the tyranny which had held other civilizations together in the past, but obsessed by the idea that if it forgot its ideals the British Empire would follow these other civilizations into dust. Carthage (p. 45), Tyre and later, almost certainly, Venice had a symbolic significance for Turner as warnings of the decline that would overtake Britain if she did not look to her moral and spiritual health. For the frontispiece of his "Liber Studiorum" he chose to represent Tyre at sunset with the Rape of Europa—a parable of the future decay of Europe in terms of the decay of Tyre, its beauty passing away into terror and judgement.

However, in thinking as he did of categories, Turner did not necessarily intend to keep the categories distinct; on the contrary, by combining features from two or more different categories in the same work he could add to his repertoire and create new expressive possibilities.

In "The Shipwreck" (p. 25), painted in 1805, he combined the features of a seascape in the Dutch style with a historic landscape based on a strictly contemporary theme. In the year of Trafalgar the sea gripped people's minds, as the sky was to do in 1940; it was the arena of the principal victories, so far, over the French and it exacted an appalling toll in lives. Some 5,000 men, it has been calculated, were drowned at sea every year during this period, which is almost five times as many in proportion to the population as are killed in road accidents today. Turner worked out the composition of the picture by means of sketches (p. 41) with as much care as a seventeenth-century master designing a figure subject.

The illustration on p. 32 shows a different fusion of categories: "Snowstorm: Hannibal and His Army crossing the Alps", exhibited in 1812. The subject this time was based on ancient history, not on a contemporary event; the influence of the Old Masters was replaced by the memory of the artist's visit to Switzerland in 1802; the weather effect, we are told, was inspired by a storm on the Yorkshire moors which Turner saw while he was staying with his friend, Walter Fawkes.

18   (continued on page 73)

20

24

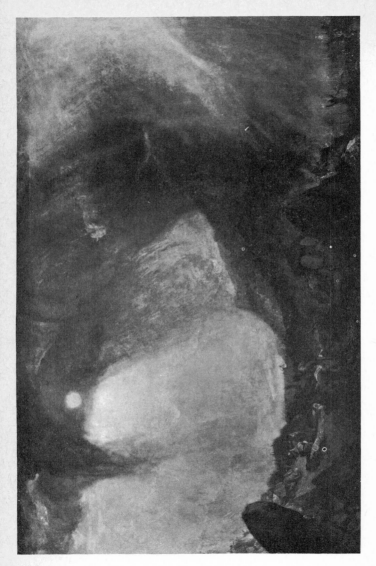

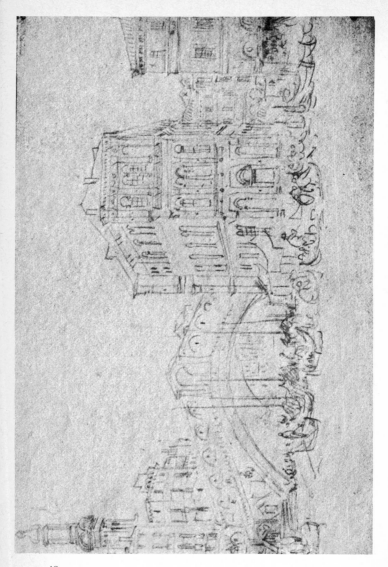

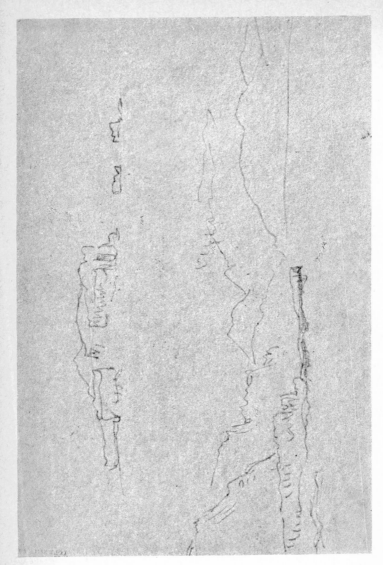

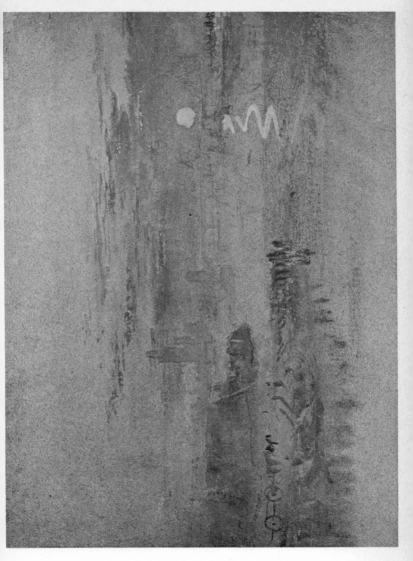

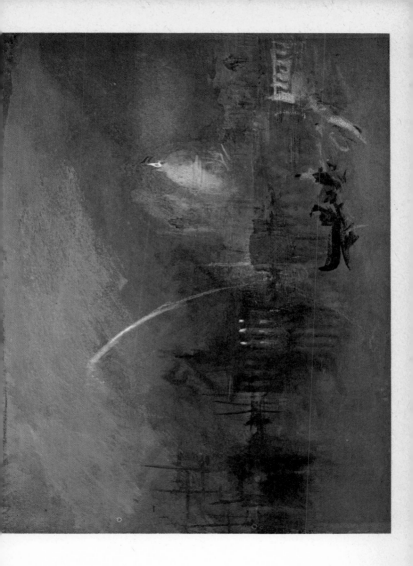

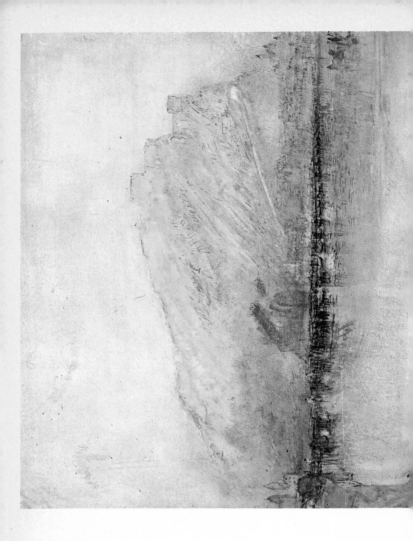

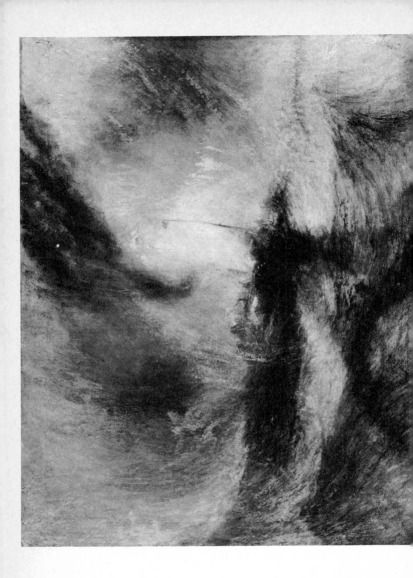

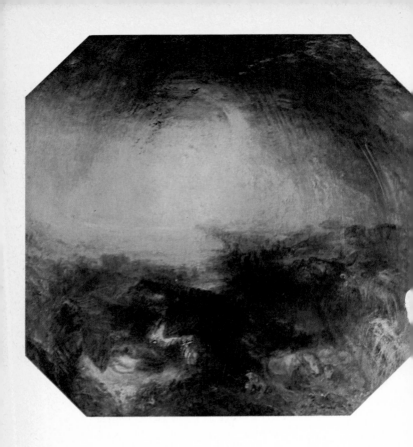

"One stormy day at Farnley," recorded Walter Fawkes's son, Hawkesworth, "Turner called to me loudly from the doorway, 'Hawkey—Hawkey!—come here—come here! Look at this thunderstorm! Isn't it grand?—isn't it wonderful?—isn't it sublime?' All this time he was making notes of its form and colour on the back of a letter. He was absorbed—he was entranced. There was the storm rolling and sweeping and shafting out its lightning over the Yorkshire hills. Presently the storm passed and he finished. 'There,' said he, 'Hawkey; in two years you will see this again, and call it Hannibal crossing the Alps.' "

Thus did Turner transform a brief but intense experience of a natural effect into one of his grandest and most imaginative canvases. It was eminently typical of his method of working. He even adapted the curving shapes, the repeated arcs of light and shade, which he had used in his early Gothic interiors—e.g. "Ewenny Priory" (p. 20), a watercolour exhibited in 1797—to express the effect of sunlight breaking through the storm clouds; the clouds seem to share the mysterious, cavernous atmosphere of the mediaeval vaults. It should be noticed, too, how the same curves are echoed in the foreground below, thereby linking the ground and the sky in a continuous pattern on the surface.

This is the first appearance in Turner's art of a compositional system he was to use again and again in later years. In using it he broke down the stable architectonic harmonies of classical landscape painting, putting in their place an unstable, shifting system of ovals and parabolas, suggestive of flux. Together with the high colour key he developed after his Italian journey, it was his most expressive pictorial device.

After a while, he began to treat the classical certainties of Claudian landscape in a similar manner. He kept the necessary identifying symbols—the Arcadian subject matter, the foreground "stage", the tall trees on either side, the view through to the horizon in the centre—but progressively eliminated the checks and balances which Claude introduced to preserve the

stability and harmony of his compositions. In Claude's paintings, no one element is allowed to dominate at the expense
of its opposite. The forms are soft enough to blend with the
atmosphere, yet not so soft that they lose their identity as
forms; the detail is clearly defined yet not so loaded that it
obscures the structure of the composition; conversely, the
composition is firm enough to hold the picture together, yet
not so firm that it appears rigid or obtrusive.

Turner undermined this delicately poised system. Already in a
comparatively early work such as "Crossing the Brook" of
1815 (pp. 28, 29) — a painting which might be described as an
English landscape in Claudian dress — one can observe this
process in operation. All the forms, especially the trees on the
left, have been extended and flattened out. The tall tree trunks
soar up from the ground, the leaves are splayed out against the
sky, the branches wave softly in the still air; the effect is almost
that of a fountain or water-spout. At the same time, the details
have lost their precision and the spatial intervals between the
various parts of the composition have become unclear. The
observer cannot "walk in the landscape and count the miles,"
as Wilson said one could in Claude's pictures. An impression
of spaciousness has been substituted for a sense of contained
space. In a word, the classical precision of Claude has been dis-
solved, to be replaced by a romantic vagueness.

These tendencies become more obvious in the ideal landscapes
painted by Turner after his visit to Italy in 1819. The first of
such landscapes was the "Bay of Baiae, with Apollo and the
Sibyl" (p. 31), exhibited in 1823. It is scarcely more than an
abstract of a Claudian composition, so far has Turner departed
from the classical harmony of paintings by Claude. The
dominant forms are swinging oval curves: the curve of the bay,
the curve formed by the dark shadow which sweeps across the
foreground and continues in the tree-trunks on the right, the
two solid ovals of the foliage of these trees.

This is an art of simplification and reduction. The complexities
and solid forms of traditional ideal landscape have been dissolv-

ed until only the bare symbols, suspended in a haze of light and colour, remain.

"The Golden Bough" (p. 56), painted in 1834, shows the process carried a stage further still. From the vocabulary of Claudian landscape Turner here makes use of only a single tree on the right—its trunk now thin and delicate and its foliage poised like a flower on a stalk—a simple dark foreground, a group of small classical figures, some counter-balancing trees, even thinner, on the left, and a view of distant water and hills on the horizon.

In such landscapes as these he seems to be trying to find out how much of the traditional apparatus of ideal landscape painting can be eliminated without abandoning landscape altogether. (In fact there is reason to believe that Turner became more critical of Claude in the latter part of his career than he had been earlier and it is significant that he dropped the "Backgrounds" lecture from his perspective series after about 1816. The years 1807-18 were the period when Claude's influence on his work was strongest. After his visit to Italy he felt free of that influence —and of the influence of the Old Masters generally— though he never abandoned their ideals.)

However, if an extremely loose and simple pictorial structure is the most obvious negative feature of Turner's later works, this is balanced by their greatest positive characteristic—their brilliance of light and colour. It is now time to examine this, but before doing so it is necessary to give more attention than has been given so far to his attitude towards nature.

That Turner was possessed by the Romantic attachment to nature—its power, its mystery and beauty—there can be no doubt. He was exhilarated by nature's violence, as has been seen from his reaction to Switzerland on his first foreign tour and to the storm at Farnley which inspired "Hannibal crossing the Alps." He was equally excited by storms at sea. It must never be forgotten that Turner began his career as a devotee of the picturesque. This coloured his view of natural scenery all his life.

On those ceaseless tours which he made all over the British Isles, and later over much of the Continent, he would always take a supply of sketchbooks with him. Whenever the coach stopped, out would come his pencil; it would move rapidly over the paper; as many as half-a-dozen sketches would be born. In the evening at his hotel he might work up a few of them in watercolours. On his return to London he would settle down and produce a whole series of finished water-colours for sale or translation into engravings (or both).

"Picturesque Views on the Southern Coast of England" (the first series, 1814-26); "The History of Richmondshire" (1818-23); "The Rivers of England" (1823-27—example on p. 33); "Picturesque Views in England and Wales" (1827-38); "The Rivers of France" (1833-35—examples on pp. 54, 55, 57)— these are some of the more important titles (the dates are those of the engravings). Generally, the engravings would be accompanied by a descriptive text and the whole enterprise would be handled by a publisher; that is to say, Turner would contract to make so many finished drawings and supervise the execution of the engravings, but would not assume financial responsibility. From the "Rivers of England" series onwards, the plates were often produced by the newly-invented process of engraving on steel instead of copper. This made it possible for a larger number of impressions to be pulled before the plate wore out, and Turner took immense trouble to train the engravers to reproduce the light-effects he obtained in his preparatory water-colours (cf. pp. 54, 55).

Even in Italy, at least on his first tour in 1819-20, Turner's attitude was that of the picturesque tourist. He did not linger over the famous monuments or produce beautiful evocative drawings of views hallowed by their associations with Horace and Virgil, as John Robert Cozens had done. Nor did he go to Italy, like Wilson, to steep himself in the countryside which had inspired Claude and by this means enrich his Claudian pictures; on the contrary, Turner's later ideal landscapes in the manner of Claude owed very little to his new-found knowledge of the country they were supposed to represent. A quick, intense view was enough; then he would pass on to the next subject. Turner is one of the ancestors of the modern tourist with a camera, who accumulates quantities of colour-transparencies, then shows them on a screen to his friends on his return.

If, then, the impression has so far been given that nature was only of secondary importance to Turner by comparison with his interest in the Old Masters, this must now be corrected; or rather, it must be shown how the two interests were reconciled in Turner's art and how the study of the past and the study of nature complemented each other. The starting point for the discussion of this problem is a series of oil sketches which Turner painted, mainly in the Thames valley, between about 1807 and 1812.

These sketches can be divided into two groups: one, a series painted on thin wooden panels, fairly small in size, on a brown ground (p. 27); the other, a group of larger sketches executed on canvas, using a white ground (p. 42). Both groups are alike in being handled lightly and summarily with broad strokes of the brush in very thin paint which has been well diluted with oil medium. The colours throughout are subdued and the subjects—a stretch of common, trees overhanging a river, a meadow with buildings in the distance—generally seen from a near viewpoint.

Of the sketches on canvas, Turner's executor, Mr. Trimmer, wrote: "Till you have seen these sketches you know nothing of his powers. There are about two score of these large subjects, rolled up, and now national property. In my judgement these are among his very finest productions: no retouching, everything firmly in its place." Trimmer added that he remembered his father telling him that Turner had painted them on the river from a boat. (This cannot, however, be entirely true, because some appear to be unfinished pictures, or preparatory studies for pictures, and must have been painted in the studio.)

More recent writers have also given these sketches high praise. In their direct and vivid rendering of the thing seen they have been said to anticipate Constable by almost ten years. What has not been properly pointed out, however, is that they are exceptional, rather than typical, in Turner's *oeuvre*. According to Thornbury, "Turner never sketched much in oil; he always got the colour too brown..." He did, it is true, produce a further group of oil sketches in the late 1820's, depicting yachts racing in the Solent (though these were possibly not done from nature); he also painted some studies of sea and sky in oils on paper. What is more, he evidently made use of the "Thames" sketches when painting a series of calm, naturalistic pictures of familiar scenery in or about 1810; "The Thames at Eton" reproduced on p. 43 is an example.

Generally speaking, however, Turner seems not only to have disliked sketching from nature in oil, but to have been anxious to keep the functions of "nature study" and "finished picture" apart. Excepting the "Thames" group just mentioned, he rarely tried to carry over the qualities of freshness and immediacy which his sketches possessed into his formal paintings. A comparison between the brilliant group of studies in opaque watercolour on blue paper which he made at or near Petworth in the early 1830's (pp. 36, 37) with "Petworth Park" or "The Old Chain Pier, Brighton" (pp. 35, 34), will serve to illustrate this; the former are studies from nature and are purely spontaneous, the latter are studies for pictures which the artist executed in his studio, having conceived them from the start in idealized terms.

Turner, that is to say, was never really bitten with that idea which runs like a *leitmotiv* throughout nineteenth-century art from Constable to Cézanne, of recreating as directly as possible on canvas his "petite sensation devant la nature." For him, rather, Nature had to be transformed into Art; and he regarded the study of Nature as at least as much a mental process as one that could be recorded directly in visual terms. On the other hand, it was a process that was very intense. As he wrote in the margin of his copy of Opie's *Lectures on Painting*: "He that has that ruling enthusiasm which accompanies abilities cannot look superficially. Every glance is a glance for study; ... Every look at nature is a refinement upon art. Each tree and blade of grass or flower is not to him the individual tree, grass or flower, but what it is in relation to the whole, its tone, its contrast and its use, and how far practicable: admiring Nature by the power and practicability of his Art, and judging of his Art by the perceptions drawn from Nature."

It was thus that Turner succeeded in evolving that imaginative reconstruction of nature which is the hallmark of all his mature work. On the one hand, as Ruskin put it, "his peculiar character, as distinguished from all other artists, was in always drawing from memories of things seen." Leaving aside the slur on "all other artists," this statement is true and important. What is more, it corresponds to our knowledge of Turner's own intentions. The truth of impression, as opposed to the truth of mere outward appearances, was something he was always anxious to preserve.

"What, do you not know yet, at your age", he once told a slow-witted fellow artist, "that you ought to paint your impressions?" And as he said of "Snowstorm: Steamboat off a Harbour's Mouth" (p. 68): "I did not paint it to be understood, but I wished to show what such a scene was like."

On the other hand, it must be remembered that Turner's interpretation of nature was intimately related to his study of the Old Masters. His historic landscapes were poetic paintings, but so were his picturesque views (pp. 33, 54) and such paintings as "Staffa: Fingal's Cave" (p. 53). It has sometimes been said that his attachment to the Old Masters was a hindrance to the development of his own style. But this is false; in fact, the reverse is the case. It was through studying the past that Turner discovered the possibilities of imaginative painting. The past gave him not only a vocabulary of style; it also supplied him with an example of what breath-taking visions the language of art could express. Having learnt these lessons and combined them with his own observations of nature, he could apply them to compositions of his own invention.

"Staffa: Fingal's Cave" (p. 53) is one of the best, and one of the best preserved, of Turner's later seascapes. It was based on the experience of a trip he made to the cave by steamboat in 1831. On the way back, "the sun, getting towards the horizon, burst through the rain-cloud, angry and for wind." A few hurried pencil sketches (p. 52) were sufficient to recall the scene to his mind. The treatment of the sea is unique; no sea quite like it had ever been painted before, containing as it does an effect of fine rain scudding across the surface of the brown water.

The composition takes up the method first used in "Hannibal crossing the Alps." There is no careful pictorial architecture underpinning the picture, but a simple, free, non-geometric pattern of curves and shapes which holds the surface loosely but effectively together. The elements are completely interfused: sea, air and dry land are merged directly into one another.

"The Rivers of France" (pp. 55, 57) were also based on very summary pencil sketches. In the finished watercolours Turner sometimes remained fairly faithful to the actual proportions of the places he was illustrating; at other times he departed radically from them. By this stage his mind could expand the slightest notation. The watercolours themselves are minutely executed and quite small in size ($5\frac{3}{4} \times 7\frac{1}{2}$ in.), but they are among his most imaginative productions. The colours marvellously express the effect of sunlight glittering on hillsides, buildings and water. It is as if Turner is rendering not so much the surfaces of forms illuminated by light as the dazzle of light itself. He was to do the same, even more magically, in his oil paintings and watercolours of Venice.

Turner's adoption of a very high colour key is the outstanding characteristic of his later work. It is usually and rightly associated with his first visit to Italy in 1819, although hints of it can be found much earlier in his career. The Continent had once more been closed to English travellers from 1803 to 1815, owing to the renewal of war with France; in the years immediately following the final defeat of Napoleon, Turner was too busy with his "History of Richmondshire" and other series of English picturesque views to make a long journey abroad. However, in July 1819 he was at last able to set out for Italy. He travelled across France and over the Mont Cenis Pass to Turin, then went to Lake Como and Venice (where he stayed a fortnight) and from there moved to Rome and Naples, returning to London on the 1st February 1820.

Much of his activity took the form of more or less careful drawings of street scenes and buildings (pp. 48, 50); as after his Swiss tour of 1802, he was only able to absorb the new discoveries he had made into the mainstream of his work after a considerable delay. He did, however, make a few very original, very simple watercolours of Venice in 1819 (p. 49), using only transparent washes of pure colour and relying on reflections in water to join sea, buildings and sky. This was to be typical of his late watercolour style, just as Venice itself was to be, in a sense, the most vital inspiration of all to him during his last years.

After a pause of nearly ten years he began producing oil paintings of the city. He also went there two or three times again: possibly in 1832, certainly in 1835 and 1840. Venice, one feels, had an emotional significance for him comparable to that of Carthage in earlier years; it was another instance of the fate of Empire. Indeed, the final extinction of the Venetian Republic by Napoleon's troops in 1798 meant much, not only to Turner himself but to his whole generation—to Byron, to Wordsworth and later, after Turner's death, to Ruskin. The once great city, Queen of the Adriatic, mistress of the Levant and upholder of western civilization, was now merely a stamping-ground for tourists and a province of the Austrian Empire. She represented, like Carthage, a warning of the fate that might one day overtake the British Empire too.

Artistically, Turner treated Venice in an entirely new way. He discarded the topographical approach of Canaletto and Guardi in favour of a method that brought representations of the city

81

into the realm of poetic painting. The famous buildings—the Dogana, the church of Santa Maria della Salute, the church of S. Giorgio, the Doges' Palace—are poised as in a mirage between sea and sky (p. 65). The shimmering reflections in the water make vertical strokes in a compositional system which has no foreground—and hence no firm base—of any kind.

To create a pattern of light and colour independent of solid objects was the great endeavour of Turner's last years. And in order to extract the utmost from it, he sought out as many situations as possible in which light and fleeting weather effects took on visible form; that is to say, in which they were not merely media through which objects might be seen but entities which became visible in themselves. Hence we find Turner depicting not only effects of strong sunlight, but snow, rain, steam (p. 71), storms of all kinds (p. 68), moonlight, fireworks (p. 61) and fire (p. 59). He also conducted several theoretical experiments, painting two pictures illustrating Goethe's *Farbenlehre* (p. 72), which he had read in English translation in 1840, and spending part of his spare time in the studio of a photographer named Mayall in order to increase his knowledge of optics.

Finally, among the watercolours he produced on one of his last tours to the Continent in 1841 were two representing the same place—the fortress of Ehrenbreitstein above Coblenz (pp. 66, 67)—from almost the same viewpoint, but painted under different conditions of light, one pink, one yellow, thus anticipating Monet's experiments with haystacks and the façade of Rouen cathedral by some fifty years. Ruskin wrote of these last Continental watercolours that they were "of the finest quality of pure Turnerian art, which is in sum . . . the true abstraction of the colour of nature as a distinct subject of study."

In the last twenty years of Turner's life there can be no doubt that his stylistic range tended to contract. The widely differing styles which he had used earlier converged as he began to treat every category of subject by the same stylistic means: compare the use of the "bow" formation, for instance, in both the watercolour of "Storm Clouds over Sea" (p. 58) and the oil painting of "Keelmen Heaving in Coals by Moonlight" (p. 59).

Similarly, his oil paintings and watercolours often became almost indistinguishable from one another since both were executed in thin transparent colours on a white ground. A mirage of light and colour—blues, pinks and yellows dissolving into one another in an opalescent haze—is the dominant pictorial theme. But he never lost touch with reality altogether; the outline of a hill, a tree, a boat or a building can always be dimly perceived.

He was very lonely during his last years. Walter Fawkes had died in 1827, his own father in 1829, Sir Thomas Lawrence in 1830 and the greatest of all his friends and patrons, Lord Egremont of Petworth House, in 1837. Many of his pictures were the debris of experiment and never left his studio while he was alive. He was persistently misunderstood even, or perhaps especially, by Ruskin, who had come to his aid, publishing *Modern Painters* (first volume 1843, the second 1846) in an attempt to vindicate his later work. He died in 1851 at the age of seventy-six, an embittered man; even after his death the ambiguous wording of his will enabled his relatives to upset its main financial provisions. But he was buried in St. Paul's Cathedral with all the leading artists of England in attendance.

He had been one of the most original figures in British art and certainly its most comprehensive genius. Any third- or fourth-rate landscape dating from the mid-nineteenth century that one comes across in a boarding house or junk shop is as likely as not to be an imitation of Turner's work. But his influence, though great, was uncreative; no one in his own time could use it as a point of departure—that is, to create something new. As was suggested at the beginning, it has only been in much more recent times that Turner has, as it were, come into his own. His art was too firmly rooted in the eighteenth century, on the one hand, and too abstract, on the other, to be in tune with later nineteenth-century developments. His treatment of light and colour was unsystematic and subjective, whereas that of the Impressionists was objective and analytic. His compositions, like theirs, showed a remarkable freedom from earlier conventions of picture-making, but his had none of that sharpness and immediacy, that down-to-earth quality, which the later nineteenth century admired. He went so far beyond the logic of appearances that there is, even now, something about his work which remains incommunicable to us.

Although no one would suggest that Turner has had a direct influence on the development of recent American painting, and although his attachment to reality, however tenuous it eventually became, separates his work from that of modern abstract artists, there is an affinity between such paintings as "Seascape" (p. 69) and paintings by Rothko and Gottlieb that can sometimes be surprisingly close. In the work of all three artists we find the same overall treatment of the surface, the same tendency to concentrate the interest in the centre of the composition at the expense of the edges, the same deployment of a loose, simple pictorial structure held lightly within the frame. There is even a partial similarity in the treatment of space—that is to say, a suggestion of space is created in front of, as well as behind, the surface of the canvas. Even if these affinities with modern painting are only apparent, not real, they are worth mentioning; they help us to appreciate, more clearly than has been possible before, the astounding originality and beauty of Turner's later work.

THE TURNER BEQUEST

The main provisions of Turner's will were two, *viz*., (1) that his personal property, valued at nearly £140,000 at his death, should be sold to provide a charitable institution for "Poor and Decayed Male Artists born in England and of English Parents only and lawful issue", and (2) that his pictures, sketches and drawings remaining in his studio should be bequeathed to the nation, to be kept together in a special gallery built for the purpose.

The first provision was frustrated by his next-of-kin (to whom he wished to leave nothing) on a legal technicality; they were enabled to inherit the entire property themselves. The gallery for the pictures was never built; but after a delay of almost ten years the National Gallery, London, was given charge of the whole collection (the "Turner Bequest"). This amounted in all to over a hundred finished pictures, some 250 unfinished pictures and oil sketches, and over 19,000 watercolours and drawings. According to the present arrangement, a small selection of the pictures is kept and exhibited at the National Gallery; the Tate Gallery holds, and exhibits a large proportion of, the remaining works in oil; the British Museum retains the watercolours and drawings.

LIST OF ILLUSTRATIONS

The illustrations are in approximate chronological order from pp. 19-37 inclusive (except that "Bligh Sand" on p. 30 and "Hannibal Crossing the Alps" on p. 32 are out of place); next there is a parallel series, mainly of drawings and watercolours, on pp. 38-53; finally, the illustrations on pp. 54-72 again continue chronologically, starting from the point where both the previous series ended.

49 VENICE: VIEW OF S. GIORGIO
1819; watercolour; $8\frac{7}{8} \times 11\frac{3}{8}$ in.;
British Museum, London

50 ROME: THE ARCH OF TITUS
1819; pencil on grey-tinted paper; $9 \times 14\frac{1}{2}$ in.;
British Museum, London

51 VIEW OF TIVOLI
1819; watercolour; 10×16 in.; British Museum, London

52 STUDY FOR "STAFFA: FINGAL'S CAVE"
1831; pencil; $4\frac{1}{2} \times 7\frac{3}{8}$ in.; British Museum, London

53 STAFFA: FINGAL'S CAVE
1832; oil on canvas; 36×48 in.;
The Hon. Gavin Astor, London

54 VIEW OF HARFLEUR
1834; steel engraving by J. Cousen; $3\frac{3}{4} \times 5\frac{1}{4}$ in.;
From the watercolour by Turner illustrated on p. 55

55 VIEW OF HARFLEUR
About 1834; watercolour and body-colour on blue paper;
$5\frac{3}{4} \times 7\frac{1}{2}$ in.; British Museum, London

56 THE GOLDEN BOUGH
1834; oil on canvas; $41\frac{1}{2} \times 64\frac{1}{2}$ in.;
Tate Gallery, London

57 THE SCARLET SUNSET
About 1834; watercolour and body-colour on blue paper;
$5\frac{3}{4} \times 7\frac{1}{2}$ in.; British Museum, London

58 STORM CLOUDS OVER SEA
After 1830; body-colour on blue-grey paper; $7\frac{1}{2} \times 10\frac{3}{4}$ in.;
British Museum, London

59 KEELMEN HEAVING IN COALS BY MOONLIGHT
1835; oil on canvas; $36\frac{1}{4} \times 48\frac{1}{4}$ in.;
National Gallery of Art, Widener Collection, Washington (D.C.)

60 SOUTHERN LANDSCAPE WITH AN AQUEDUCT
After 1830; oil on canvas; $58\frac{3}{4} \times 98\frac{1}{2}$ in.;
Tate Gallery, London

61 VENICE: THE SALUTE AND THE DOGANA BY NIGHT
1835 or 1840; watercolour and chalks on brown paper;
$9\frac{1}{2} \times 12\frac{1}{4}$ in.; British Museum, London

62 NORHAM CASTLE
After 1830; oil on canvas; $35\frac{1}{2} \times 47\frac{1}{2}$ in.;
Tate Gallery, London

63 INTERIOR AT PETWORTH
1830–37; oil on canvas; $35\frac{3}{4} \times 47\frac{1}{4}$ in.;
Tate Gallery, London

64 THE FIGHTING "TÉMÉRAIRE" TUGGED TO HER LAST BERTH
1839; oil on canvas; $35\frac{3}{4} \times 48$ in.;
National Gallery, London

65 VENICE: THE DOGANA AND S. GIORGIO
1842; oil on canvas; $24\frac{1}{4} \times 36\frac{1}{2}$ in.;
Tate Gallery, London

66 THE "PINK" EHRENBREITSTEIN
About 1841; watercolour; $9\frac{3}{4} \times 11\frac{7}{8}$ in.;
British Museum, London

67 THE "YELLOW" EHRENBREITSTEIN
About 1841; watercolour; $9\frac{1}{2} \times 11\frac{3}{8}$ in.;
British Museum, London

68 SNOWSTORM: STEAMBOAT OFF A HARBOUR'S MOUTH
1842; oil on canvas; $35\frac{1}{2} \times 47\frac{1}{2}$ in.;
National Gallery, London

69 SEASCAPE
About 1840–45; oil on canvas; $35\frac{3}{4} \times 48$ in.;
Tate Gallery, London

70 BADEN, SWITZERLAND
1844; watercolour; $9 \times 12\frac{7}{8}$ in.;
British Museum, London

71 RAIN, STEAM AND SPEED – THE GREAT WESTERN RAILWAY
1844; oil on canvas; $35\frac{3}{4} \times 48$ in.;
National Gallery, London

72 SHADE AND DARKNESS: THE EVENING OF THE DELUGE
1843; oil on canvas; octagonal, $30\frac{1}{2} \times 30\frac{1}{2}$ in.;
Tate Gallery, London